DUEL OF THE IRONCLADS

Editor and Designer: Charles Mikolaycak   Text by Carole Kismaric

DUEL OF THE IRONCLADS
IN PICTURES BY FRED FREEMAN

1861 - 1862

TIME-LIFE BOOKS, New York

Day after day President Abraham Lincoln peered through a spyglass from his third floor office in the White House. Anxiously he looked past farmlands and grazing cows, down the Potomac River toward Chesapeake Bay. At odd hours of the day and night, his advisers found him sitting nervously in the small telegraph office in the War Department, waiting for news. It was the spring of 1861, and the United States had embarked on a long and bloody Civil War. Since Lincoln had taken office, the Union had begun to split apart on the issue of slavery. Fighting had started early one April morning when Rebel troops of the South shelled South Carolina's Fort Sumter. Six states had withdrawn from the Union and it was certain that more would follow.

Lincoln had special cause to be worried. His spies in Virginia had reported that the young Confederacy of Southern States was building a deadly new kind of warship, protected by iron sides instead of wooden ones. This ship, they said, was designed to travel up the Potomac to destroy Washington. Unharmed by cannon shot, it might continue along the coast, bombarding city after city in the North.

Lincoln knew the reports were probably true. Stephen Mallory, who was now Secretary of the Navy for the Confederacy, had been a U.S. Senator from Florida and chairman of the Senate's naval committee before the war. He had often talked to Lincoln of the great possibilities that lay in the use of ironclad ships. The President was sure that Mallory would lose no time in building an ironclad and sending it to attack Washington. It was for news of this ship that he waited and watched.

About a week after the fall of Fort Sumter, President Lincoln had announced that

the Union Navy would blockade Southern ports from Virginia to Texas. The blockade was supposed to strangle the South by stopping ships from carrying bundles of cotton to England and France, and returning with the guns and war supplies the Rebels desperately needed. But to carry out the blockade, Gideon Welles, Secretary of the Union Navy, desperately needed ships. In April of 1861, the largest single group of Union warships was at the Gosport Navy Yard in Portsmouth, Virginia. Welles knew he had to get them out of Virginia because that state was ready to join the South at any minute and the vessels might be lost. He was especially interested in the 3,500-ton steam frigate Merrimack, a big three-masted sailing ship that also had steam engines and a propeller.

Welles ordered the yard's commander, Commodore Charles McCauley, to deliver the Merrimack to safety in the port of Philadelphia. But McCauley, a Virginian, knew that Virginia might leave the Union, so he stalled, hoping to get the ship for the South. Alarmed, Welles ordered Commodore Hiram Paulding and the steamship Pawnee to relieve McCauley of his command and to tow the Merrimack to Fort Monroe, a Union stronghold 12 miles away. Paulding's instructions were to save what he could in the Navy yard, but to destroy any guns, ammunition or ships that might fall into Virginia's hands.

Paulding and the Pawnee arrived at the yard at 8 p.m. on April 20—just in time to see scuttled warships slowly sinking into the slimy Elizabeth River. McCauley, finally realizing that an angry crowd of Virginians was about to attack the yard and take it over, had instructed his men to destroy everything. Paulding relieved

As fires rage, a seaman breaks the powder train leading to kegs of explosives in the Gosport dry dock.

8   McCauley of his command and divided his men into small work parties to finish the job. The Northerners ran about the yard spreading cotton waste soaked in turpentine and laying trails of gunpowder to send fires through the wooden buildings. They attacked the yard's 1,200 heavy cannon with sledge hammers and spiked them so they would not fire. The huge stone dry dock, in which many of the Navy's ships were built and repaired, was mined with 20 kegs of powder. At 2 a.m. Paulding fired a signal rocket and all charges were ignited. The country's largest Navy yard and arsenal burst into a golden sheet of flame. But at the last minute an unidentified Union petty officer interrupted the powder trail in the dry dock. Apparently the officer did not want to see pieces of granite fall on the nearby homes of his Virginian friends. His action saved the dock. It also gave the South a way to build its dreaded iron ship.

Unluckily for the North, the dry dock was not the only valuable property that fell into Southern hands. When the Union sailors left the yard, the angry Virginians broke through the gates and put out enough fires to save millions of dollars' worth of supplies. They salvaged a large number of cannon (Paulding's men had not spiked them properly), as well as powder and shot—a priceless treasure, since the South had no factories for making these weapons of war. The Southerners also seized several large warships, including the Merrimack, which was only partially burned.

Immediately Confederate Navy Secretary Mallory began rebuilding plans. The son of a sea captain from Connecticut, he had become interested in iron ships when the French used three of them with spectacular success against the Russians in the

Black Sea during the Crimean War of 1853-1856. As a U.S. Senator, Mallory had followed later developments, including a heated race between England and France to build ironclads. The French launched the armored frigate La Gloire in 1859 and one year later the British built the Warrior. It was plain to Mallory that the age of the wooden ship was nearing its end.

At first Mallory urged the Confederacy to buy two ironclads from the Europeans, built along the lines of the Gloire, which could fight at sea. But the plan had failed. One day, as he surveyed the fire-blackened hulls in the Gosport yard, he made his decision. Let the South build her own iron ship! An iron ship to defend her harbors and perhaps even smash the Yankee blockade! The Confederacy had little money and no facilities for building new ships, but it could rebuild an old one.

Fortunately for Mallory, John Porter, a naval builder stationed at the yard, also had experience with iron ships. Some years before, Porter had designed an ironclad which the U.S. government had turned down. When Porter learned of Mallory's intentions, he drew up a plan for remodeling the Merrimack along the lines of his earlier model.

Mallory enthusiastically approved the idea. By May 30, 1861, the Merrimack had been raised from her muddy bed and moved into the undamaged dry dock. She had burned only to the waterline and her hull and machinery were still in working condition; it would not be difficult to pump her dry. Porter went to work on his final plans, measuring the big hull with a tape measure. On June 30, 1861, without waiting for official approval, Mallory gave the go-ahead to Porter's scheme.

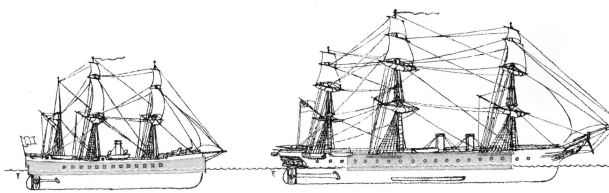

The French Gloire, first ship
to be clad with iron *(shown in gray)*

The British frigate Warrior, built with iron frames
as well as iron plating amidships

A FLOATING FORTRESS

Porter's plan was to cut down the hull of the Merrimack to the lowest level possible while still saving her machinery, which was priceless to the South. The hull was to be stripped to the top of the 17.5-foot propeller, leaving the tops of the steam boilers exposed. Above the boilers a new gun deck was to be built, and on top of this a big, tentlike fort with wooden sides two feet thick. This structure, called the casemate, was to be covered with two blankets of heavy iron strips, each two inches thick.

Porter knew the ship would be easiest to damage at the "knuckle," the joint where the bottom of the casemate met the top of the hull. The farther he could keep this joint under water, the safer it would be from enemy fire. But Southern rivers and harbors were shallow—the main channel outside the Navy Yard was at most only 24 feet deep. The hull already drew 22 feet of water. Porter knew that if he pushed the hull down more than two feet to protect the knuckle under water the ship would risk running aground.

As armament, the Merrimack was to have 10 big guns. Finally, a 1,500-pound cast-iron beak was to be bolted to the ironclad's prow—a deadly weapon for ramming holes in wooden ships.

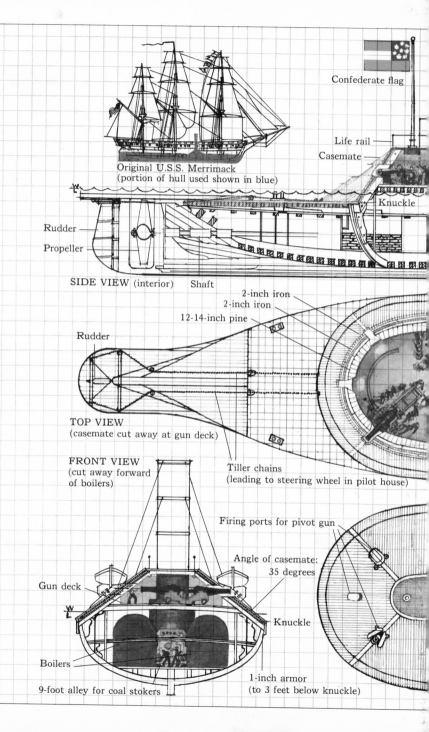

Confederate flag

Life rail

Casemate

Knuckle

Original U.S.S. Merrimack
(portion of hull used shown in blue)

Rudder

Propeller

SIDE VIEW (interior)   Shaft

2-inch iron

2-inch iron

12-14-inch pine

Rudder

TOP VIEW
(casemate cut away at gun deck)

Tiller chains
(leading to steering wheel in pilot house)

FRONT VIEW
(cut away forward
of boilers)

Firing ports for pivot gun

Angle of casemate:
35 degrees

Gun deck

Knuckle

Boilers

9-foot alley for coal stokers

1-inch armor
(to 3 feet below knuckle)

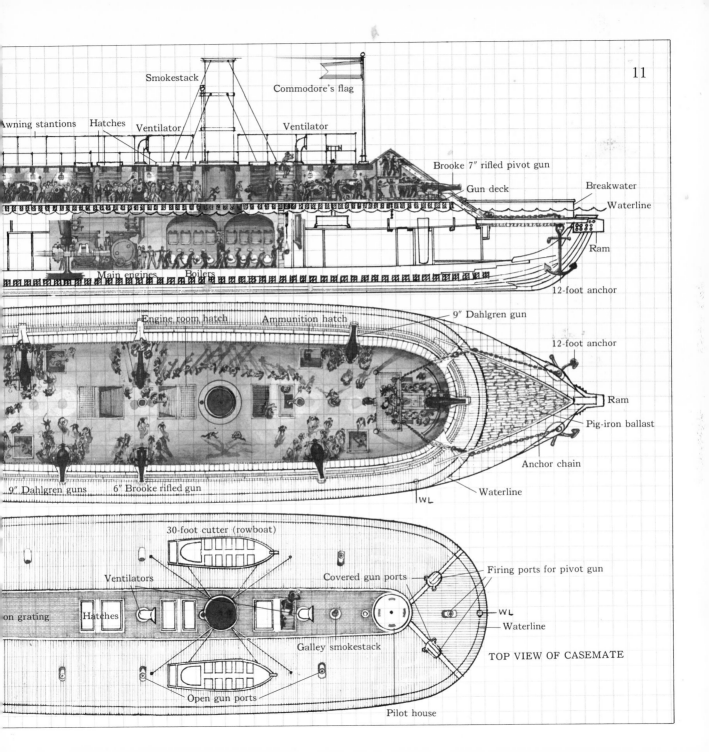

Smokestack

Commodore's flag

Awning stantions Hatches Ventilator Ventilator

Brooke 7" rifled pivot gun

Gun deck

Breakwater

Waterline

Ram

Main engines Boilers

12-foot anchor

Engine room hatch Ammunition hatch

9" Dahlgren gun

12-foot anchor

Ram

Pig-iron ballast

Anchor chain

9" Dahlgren guns 6" Brooke rifled gun

Waterline

WL

30-foot cutter (rowboat)

Covered gun ports

Firing ports for pivot gun

Ventilators

WL

on grating Hatches

Waterline

Galley smokestack

TOP VIEW OF CASEMATE

Open gun ports

Pilot house

12 During the summer work went quickly on the Merrimack. In addition to a small army of laborers, Porter had managed to round up 80 skilled shipfitters and blacksmiths, who worked until 8 o'clock every night without extra pay. Great secrecy surrounded the work. From time to time Confederate naval authorities released false information about the ship's progress just to confuse the North.

As the Merrimack took shape, the North finally awoke: to meet the threat, she would have to build an ironclad ship of her own. At the urging of Navy Secretary Gideon Welles, a board of three senior naval officers was appointed to choose designs. All of the officers were old seamen used to wooden ships; they could not believe that the "sails which whitened all the seas" were about to give way to ugly iron boats spitting smoke. After a month's investigation, they reported that wooden ships were still best for fighting in the open sea. Welles ordered them to get proposals for the ironclad vessels anyway. Advertisements were placed in newspapers and eventually 17 designs were submitted. The officers narrowed the choice to two ships; one of them was the Galena, designed by Cornelius Scranton Bushnell, a young Connecticut shipbuilder. But they were not sure that the Galena would float, so they asked Bushnell to check its soundness with other engineers. Bushnell went to one of the world's best—John Ericsson, who lived and worked in New York.

The two men met one day early in September in Ericsson's cluttered study. Bushnell was told to leave the plans and return the next day for Ericsson's decision. He was not surprised when the engineer assured him that his boat would float. But, Ericsson asked, wouldn't Bushnell like to see an unbeatable ironclad that could be

President Lincoln and Navy officers examine a model of Ericsson's ironclad.

built in only 90 days? Ericsson reached into a dusty cupboard and handed Bushnell a toylike cardboard model. It looked very much like a tin can mounted on a long, low raft. As they talked, the young builder realized that this strange design was better than his own—that, in fact, it was the Union's best chance.

Bushnell quickly took the model to Secretary Welles, who arranged a meeting with President Lincoln for 11 o'clock on September 10. At the meeting the bickering sides talked on and on. Some urged trying the ironclad ship; others laughed at it. Finally the President was asked what he thought of the plan. "All I can say," replied Lincoln, "is what the girl said when she put her foot into the stocking: 'It strikes me there's something in it.'" With this the President walked out.

Two of the three board members were ready to vote for approval, but one, Commander Charles H. Davis, stubbornly held out. Bushnell saw that he would have to get Ericsson to come to Washington himself to answer Davis' complicated questions. The old engineer, however, had sworn never to set foot in the capital again. Seventeen years before, on the trial run of a new warship, a cannon that was an imitation of one he had designed had exploded, killing two members of the President's Cabinet. Although Ericsson had not built the faulty gun, the Navy blamed him for the disaster and refused to pay him for his work. Ericsson wanted nothing more to do with the government, but Bushnell finally managed to convince him. When he appeared before the board, Ericsson thrilled every man in the room with his description of the little boat and what she could do. Within an hour, he was awarded the contract and told to go home and begin work immediately.

When he arrived in America from Sweden in 1839, John Ericsson was already an internationally famous inventor and engineer. He had built the first steam-powered fire engine, and the first warship driven by a screw propeller instead of a slow, cumbersome paddle wheel.

Ericsson put all of his genius and long experience into the design of his ship, which he named the "Monitor"—a warning to the South of the Union's military strength. He completed more than 100 drawings to guide the workmen, who had started to build the ironclad in Brooklyn, New York. Through lonely days and nights he worked in his shirt sleeves at his desk *(left),* planning every detail from the propeller to the anchor well. To save time, he simplified his original design. He also ignored the request of the Ironclad Board that the ship be designed with masts and sails as well as engines. Most of the time he took his rough drawings to the yard himself, where they went immediately into production because time was short. So great was Ericsson's drive that he often forgot to eat or sleep. The Monitor had to be finished before the Merrimack steamed out to challenge the Union fleet's blockade.

THE "TIN CAN ON A RAFT"

Ericsson's Monitor was radically different from anything that had ever sailed the seas. Her flat-bottomed iron hull sat so low in the water that she resembled a raft; this design shielded her crew and machinery underwater, almost like a submarine, offering very little target area above water for enemy gunners to hit. Her wooden deck was sheathed in armor that hung over the sides of the hull like a heavy iron skirt. This skirt was to protect the ship from hits at the waterline and from ramming by an enemy ship.

In the center of the deck was the Monitor's most original

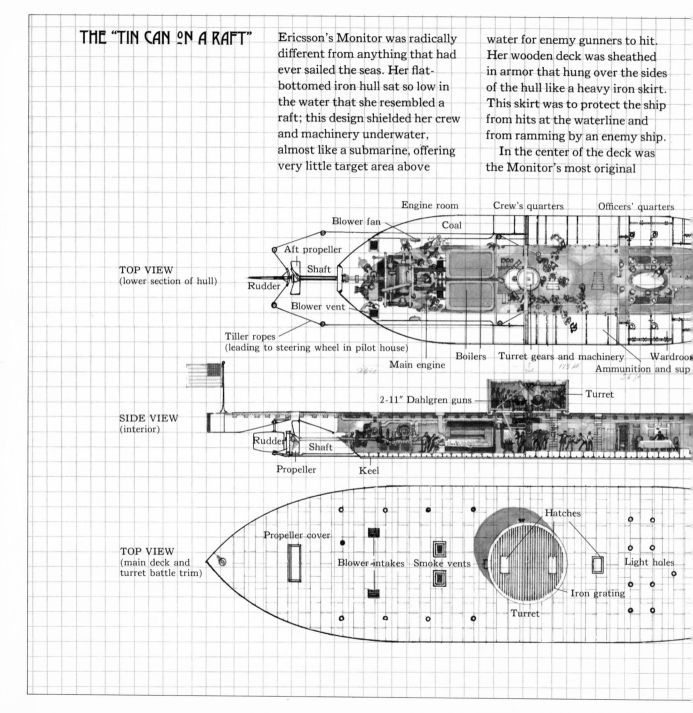

TOP VIEW
(lower section of hull)

Engine room
Blower fan
Coal
Crew's quarters
Officers' quarters
Aft propeller
Shaft
Rudder
Blower vent
Tiller ropes
(leading to steering wheel in pilot house)
Main engine
Boilers
Turret gears and machinery
Wardroo
Ammunition and sup

SIDE VIEW
(interior)

2-11″ Dahlgren guns
Turret
Rudder
Shaft
Propeller
Keel

TOP VIEW
(main deck and turret battle trim)

Propeller cover
Hatches
Blower intakes
Smoke vents
Light holes
Iron grating
Turret

feature: a revolving gun turret. This huge "tin can" was built of eight layers of iron, each one inch thick. Up to that time, when the captain of a warship wanted to aim his main guns, he had to turn his entire vessel broadside to the enemy, a slow and very clumsy maneuver. The Monitor's turret changed all this. It could move in a full circle to surprise the enemy from any angle. The ship had two very large guns, mounted side by side in the turret.

Toward the forward end of the deck was the Monitor's control center: a heavily armored pilot house projecting a little less than four feet above the deck. From this tiny forward station the captain, pilot and helmsman would direct the ship in battle.

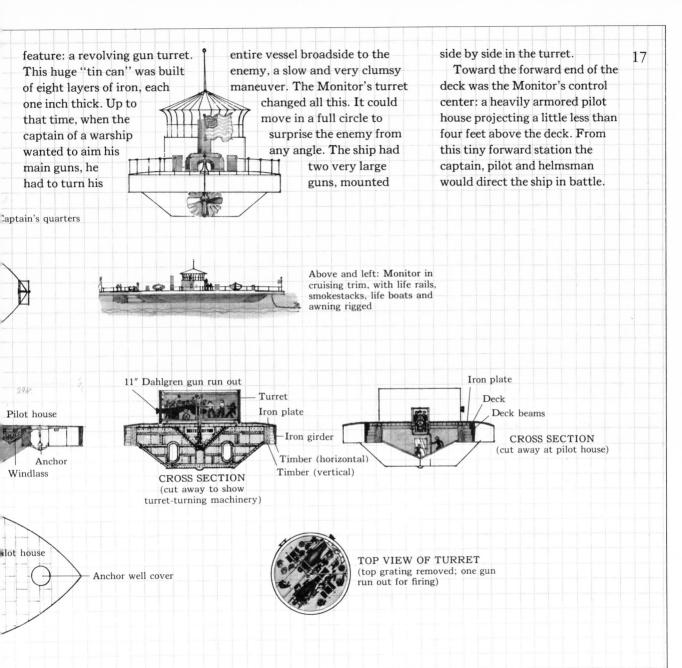

Captain's quarters

Above and left: Monitor in cruising trim, with life rails, smokestacks, life boats and awning rigged

Pilot house

Anchor
Windlass

11″ Dahlgren gun run out

Turret
Iron plate

Iron girder

Timber (horizontal)
Timber (vertical)

CROSS SECTION
(cut away to show turret-turning machinery)

Iron plate

Deck

Deck beams

CROSS SECTION
(cut away at pilot house)

Pilot house

Anchor well cover

TOP VIEW OF TURRET
(top grating removed; one gun run out for firing)

17

As Ericsson began to develop final plans for the Monitor, the South was moving along rapidly on its own ironclad. During Thanksgiving week, the first shipment of armor plates arrived by railroad and were carried on wagons to the dry dock *(right)*. At the same time the Merrimack's cannon were being lifted by a steam crane into position in the new wooden casemate. Tough riflemen guarded the ship day and night against surprise attack. No one could be trusted; spies were everywhere in the area.

The ship's new iron plates came from the Tredegar Iron Works in Richmond, Virginia, the only mill in the South capable of rolling the quantities of iron needed. To determine how thick the plates had to be, several experimental samples were made, consisting of different numbers of layers and different thicknesses of plate. Cannon were fired at each of these targets to see which stood up best. Originally Porter was going to use three one-inch layers of iron to coat the Merrimack. But the experiments showed that he needed two layers of two-inch plates. The men worked through the fall and early winter installing the armor. They were turning the South's dream into a nightmare for the Union.

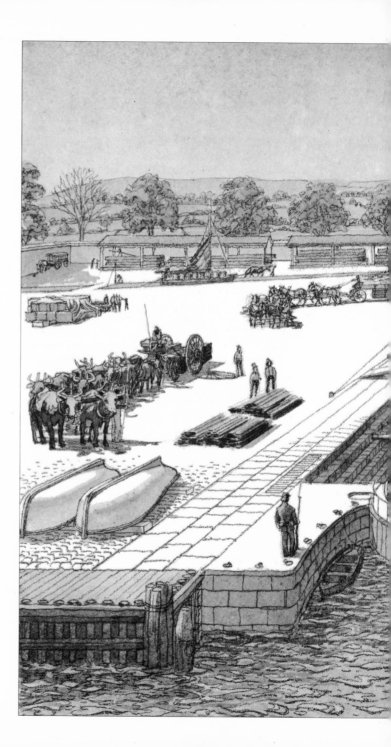

Scores of workmen swarmed around the Monitor as the job of building her progressed. Every day Ericsson visited the "shiphouse," the big shed at the Brooklyn yard, clambering up a ladder *(right)* to inspect the work and to make sure the fast pace he set was being kept. In this picture the lower part of the hull has been laid. Sticking up above it are girders to hold the deck and its heavy iron skirt. The big nine-foot propeller is ready for lowering on a hoist at left. Power for the hoists is provided by steam engines like the one just to the left of the ladder. A large-wheeled horse cart, at right, has just dragged in three heavy timbers to be used as deck planking under the armor. At the far right, blacksmiths hammer out fittings on an anvil; on deck, other workers heat rivets in a portable furnace before pounding them into place.

The iron for the Monitor was rolled at Rowland's Continental Iron Works in upstate New York and brought down by railroad to the Brooklyn yard. While the Continental Iron Works was making the iron for the hull, other factories were building the machinery and rolling the armor for the 140-ton turret. The gap in the race of the ironclads was closing inch by inch.

In the South, the patriotic ladies of Portsmouth and nearby Norfolk did their share to help equip the Merrimack. Wool, which was used to make bags to hold gun-powder, was in short supply. The editor of the Norfolk newspaper wrote a story urging the ladies to contribute any wool they had at home. They turned in flannel and woolen petticoats, dresses and skirts. These were received by Navy men working in stores in the Portsmouth-Norfolk area *(right)*.

The guns in which the powder bags were to be used were designed by Lieutenant John Brooke. He took six Dahlgren smoothbore cannon and shrank 3-inch bands of iron around their powder chambers to withstand more powerful charges. Four new guns were cast and rifled—the insides of their barrels bored with spiraling grooves—so that they could fire shells that spun like rifle bullets for greater accuracy.

After the first shipments of iron plates had been delivered, however, the Southern builders hit a snag. The Tredegar Iron Works had accepted more war orders than it could handle; delivery of the Merrimack's iron was held up. So during the winter months, while the North moved quickly on the Monitor, work on the Merrimack dragged on.

A cold, drizzling rain fell on the morning the Monitor was to be launched. No newspapers had announced the event, but word of mouth brought hundreds of curious onlookers to the docks along the East River. Workmen and visitors made bets with each other ("She'll float like a wood raft!" "Hogwash! She'll hit bottom in three seconds!"). Excitement ran high as the last timber block was knocked away and the ship slipped down the ways toward the river. Ericsson stood proudly on her deck in company with the builder, a Navy officer and a few workmen *(right),* not caring that he might be drenched when she hit water. A small boat was stationed nearby to rescue the men in case the Monitor went under.

Then suddenly a cheer went up from the crowd. Waving hats and handkerchiefs filled the air. The little iron ship floated! She had passed her first test.

The next week the Monitor was taken to the Brooklyn Navy Yard for final fitting out and on February 27 she went on a shakedown cruise in New York Harbor. The trial run disclosed several minor problems, mainly with the steering mechanism. In the next few days, while Ericsson fixed the steering, the Merrimack neared completion in the South.

The eyes of the world were on America as the race to build the Monitor and Merrimack drew to a close. From the beginning of the war, the neutral French had sent observers to witness the struggle on the battlefields and the seas. By mid-February several French ships were stationed in Hampton Roads, near the Gosport Navy Yard.

A story in the *New York Times* had reported that the Merrimack would never get to sea. Actually, she was finished and waiting to be launched. Hoping to keep the ship's completion a secret, Confederate officials had leaked false information, which had found its way to the newspaper.

The French wanted to find out exactly what shape the Merrimack was in. So the French commmodore, the Marquis de Montaignac, requested a tour of the ship. The South agreed, hoping these visitors might influence the French government to support the Confederacy.

The tour turned into a festive occasion that lasted two days. Officers' wives and townspeople were invited aboard to entertain the visitors. By the time the Marquis and his officers departed *(left)* everyone was talking about what would happen when the Merrimack went into action.

THE IRONCLADS COMPARED

	MERRIMACK	MONITOR
Designer	John Porter	John Ericsson
Where built	Gosport Navy Yard, Portsmouth, Va.	Green Point, Brooklyn, N.Y.
Cost	$110,000	$195,142
Time to build	9 months	less than 4 months
Number in crew	350	59
Length (overall)	262.9 feet	172 feet
Beam (width)	51.2 feet	41 feet
Draft (depth in water)	22 feet	11 feet 4 inches
Displacement	3500 tons	776 tons
Speed	6 knots	8 knots
Time needed to turn full circle	30-40 minutes	5 minutes
Number of boilers	4 steam	2 steam
Propeller (diameter)	17 feet 6 inches	9 feet
Thickness of main armor	4 inches (casemate)	8 inches (turret)
Guns	2 7″ Brooke rifles	2 11″ Dahlgrens
	2 6″ Brooke rifles	
	6 9″ Dahlgrens	
Ammunition used	shell shot and hot shot	solid and shell shot
Time needed to load and fire	5 minutes	7-8 minutes

Commanding Officer

FRANKLIN BUCHANAN

Flag Officer Buchanan, known as "Old Buck," became the South's only four-star admiral.

JOHN L. WORDEN

Lieutenant Worden, an able officer, headed the U.S. Naval Academy at Annapolis after the war.

Executive Officer

CATESBY JONES

Lieutenant Jones, a midshipman at 15, was an experienced officer of 40 when he joined the ship.

S. DANA GREENE

Lieutenant Greene, a graduate of the Naval Academy, was Worden's second in command at 22.

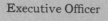

On February 24, the big valves were opened and water flooded into the dry dock at Gosport Navy Yard. The Merrimack was afloat at last. She was officially renamed the C.S.S. (Confederate States Ship) Virginia. But to her Yankee foes, and to later generations of Americans, she remained the Merrimack.

It had been difficult to assemble a crew because early in the war most Southerners had joined the army. Some seamen were found around Norfolk, and naval recruiters visited every army camp in the area to search for more. From the 200 men who volunteered, 80 were selected because they had some experience as seamen or gunners. Commanding this makeshift crew was Franklin Buchanan, a naval officer who 26 years before had helped to organize the U.S. Naval Academy at Annapolis.

During the nine months it took to get the Merrimack ready, the North had rallied. On February 25, exactly one day after the launching of the Merrimack, the U.S.S. Monitor was commissioned in the Union Navy. She had been completed in less than four months—101 working days.

Gloomy predictions about the North's "floating coffin" had not stopped her crew of 59 seamen from volunteering. Lieutenant John L. Worden was to captain her. Before his assignment to the Monitor, Worden had been captured while delivering orders to the Pensacola, Florida naval base and had spent seven months in a Confederate jail; he had recently been released in an exchange of prisoners of war.

In each case, the ship and its crew were strangers to each other. There had been little chance for the men to "work" the vessels—to learn their strengths and weaknesses. But time had run out; the moment had come for action.

30 On Thursday, March 6, the Monitor put to sea. Her orders were to proceed to Hampton Roads, where the Union fleet lay anchored blockading Portsmouth, Norfolk and the James River. Here she would be given orders for her final destination. The Navy's plan was to send the Monitor and three wooden ships up the Potomac River to protect Washington. The arrival of the new ironclad in the Roads was also intended to cheer Fort Monroe's worn-out troops, who had spent a cold, wretched winter manning the advance base for Northern troops.

A tugboat, the Seth Low, towed the Monitor out of New York harbor at 11 a.m., accompanied by two gunboats. The sea was smooth, the breeze gentle and the sky unusually fair for March. For the first 24 hours all went well. Then at noon on Friday, March 7, the wind changed. For the next three days, the men of the Monitor lived what must have seemed like a thousand years.

The little iron boat had not been designed for rough ocean water. When the wind increased, the sea was whipped into heavy waves. The ship's low deck was constantly awash with water. As the engines clanked along, the waves crashed against the ship with such force that water entered under the turret. Workers at the Navy yard had not believed Ericsson when he had assured them that the turret would be watertight. They had placed a hemp rope in between the turret and the circular bronze track on which it ran, thinking this would act like weather stripping to help keep the water out. Unhappily, it did just the opposite. Water also poured through the sight holes in the pilot house with such force that it knocked the helmsman from his position at the wheel. Waves slopped down the blower pipes that provided the engines with air,

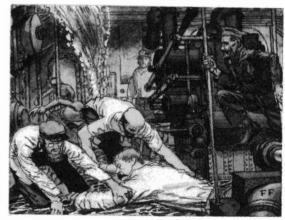

As the Monitor's engine room fills with water, Paymaster William Keeler (left) and a crewman rescue Assistant Chief Engineer Isaac Newton, who has passed out from fumes.

stopping the blower fans and the engines as well. The Monitor was helpless, with no
power, in the middle of a raging sea—a situation neither her builder nor her inexperienced crew had ever expected. Suffocating fumes from the engines soon filled the engine room, choking the crewmen there; several men had to be dragged to the top of the turret to revive in the fresh air. Finally, the hand pumps broke down. It was useless to bail; the water was entering too quickly. This is it, thought Lieutenant Worden; the Monitor was going to sink after all! But by some miracle the wind and the seas subsided. By evening the exhausted men had repaired damage, gotten the engines started and were underway again.

Lieutenant Samuel Dana Greene, the executive officer, took the next watch so that Worden, the tired captain, could catch some sleep. At midnight, Greene was relieved by another officer. As he lay down on his bunk for a nap, he was startled by a loud noise. The wheel ropes, which turned the rudder, had jammed. Water poured into the ship as she floundered in the waves; the blowers and engines failed and the ordeal began all over. It was not until 8 o'clock the following morning that the Monitor and her crew were out of danger.

The men had spent almost two days fighting a leaking ship, choking fumes, seasickness and their own fear. They were exhausted from keeping the Monitor afloat. There had only been time for some hard sea biscuits, cheese and water. No one had slept in 48 hours. The men's spirits were low as they sailed into Chesapeake Bay on the afternoon of March 8. Then suddenly they heard gunshots and looked into a sky filled with smoke and black puffs from exploding shells.

Control of Hampton Roads—the body of water shown in the map at right—was vital to both sides. Ninety-nine miles up the James River from the Roads lay Richmond, the Confederate capital. One hundred and seventy miles from the Roads, up the Potomac, lay Washington. If either side could attack and seize the other's major city, it might win the war then and there. Between the Union forces at Hampton Roads and Richmond there was only a small army of Southern troops. George McClellan, the Union commander, wanted to move his troops and supplies by water up the James River to Richmond, bypassing the Southern soldiers. But when he learned that the Merrimack was being built at Portsmouth, he abandoned the plan. McClellan, by a strange coincidence, had been an observer in the Crimean War that so interested Mallory, and had seen the destruction the French ironclads caused. The general greatly feared what the South's iron ship might do.

Hampton Roads in early March was surrounded by Northern and Southern forces. The South held all positions on the southern bank: the cities of Norfolk and Portsmouth, and gun batteries at Sewell's Point, Craney Island and Pig Point (marked by Confederate flags on the map). The South also had three small warships imprisoned up the James River; the larger Union ships and guns at Newport News prevented them from coming down into the Roads. The North held positions on the northern bank (Union flags), including strongholds at Fort Monroe and the Rip Raps, a gun position built on rocks in the channel; the Merrimack would have to pass between these if she were to head out of the Roads toward Washington. In most places there were only three to four miles separating the two sides.

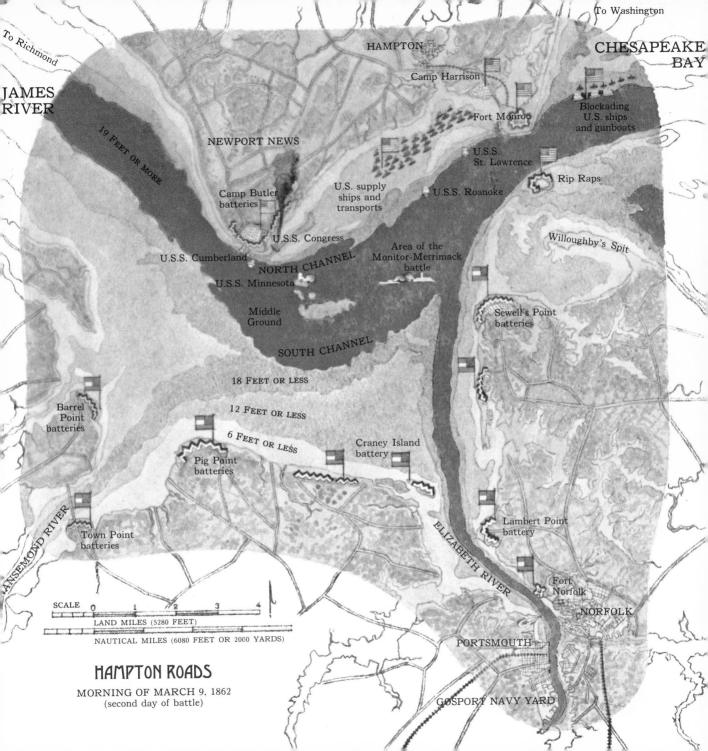

To Washington

To Richmond

HAMPTON

CHESAPEAKE
BAY

JAMES
RIVER

Camp Harrison

Blockading
U.S. ships
and gunboats

19 FEET OR MORE

Fort Monroe

NEWPORT NEWS

U.S.S.
St. Lawrence

Rip Raps

Camp Butler
batteries

U.S. supply
ships and
transports

U.S.S. Roanoke

U.S.S. Congress

Area of the
Monitor-Merrimack
battle

Willoughby's Spit

U.S.S. Cumberland

NORTH CHANNEL

U.S.S. Minnesota

Middle
Ground

Sewell's Point
batteries

SOUTH CHANNEL

18 FEET OR LESS

12 FEET OR LESS

Barrel
Point
batteries

6 FEET OR LESS

Pig Point
batteries

Craney Island
battery

Lambert Point
battery

ANSEMOND RIVER

ELIZABETH RIVER

Town Point
batteries

Fort
Norfolk

SCALE   0   1   2   3   4

NORFOLK

LAND MILES (5280 FEET)

NAUTICAL MILES (6080 FEET OR 2000 YARDS)

PORTSMOUTH

HAMPTON ROADS

MORNING OF MARCH 9, 1862
(second day of battle)

GOSPORT NAVY YARD

34   A little before noon on March 8, while the Monitor was fighting for her life on the ocean, the Merrimack steamed slowly out of Gosport Navy Yard, followed by two small gunboats, the Beaufort and the Raleigh *(right)*. The sides of the ironclad had been sloshed with buckets of pork fat so that the enemy's cannon shot would glance off without doing damage. The crew was lined up smartly on top of the casemate; a seaman at the bow flung his lead bob to sound the depth of the channel ahead. The banks of the Elizabeth River were crowded with townspeople and with farmers on their way into Norfolk and Portsmouth with products to sell. The Southerners cheered and waved at the big iron vessel as it made its way downstream.

From the very beginning the Merrimack's crew could see that their ship was sluggish and steered badly. They worked the engines carefully to avoid any accident on the way to Hampton Roads, 10 miles away. The Chief Engineer, H. Ashton Ramsey, reported of the ship that the men had "very little confidence in her." They had said goodbye to their families and sweethearts and had paid their last visits to church. Few men believed they would actually return home.

Flag Officer Buchanan, the

Merrimack's commander, had decided to test his new ship first on the Union warships Cumberland and Congress, which lay off the Union shore batteries at Newport News. After exchanging fire with the Union ships, damaging one and setting the other on fire, Buchanan moved off to a distance of a mile —enough to gather speed for his deadliest maneuver. He passed the word: "Stand fast. We're going to ram." The Merrimack slowly bore down on the Cumberland, smashing into the side of the wooden ship and opening a huge hole. The shock of the collision echoed through the iron ship. As she backed away her cast iron ram twisted off in the side of her victim. The Cumberland, sinking, fired three broadsides point-blank into the Merrimack *(left)*, shaking her and carrying away a lifeboat, railings and an anchor chain. But the ironclad ship passed the test: her armor, though cracked, held.

Meanwhile, the Congress had been towed aground in shallow water to escape the Merrimack's ram. The ironclad blasted away at her and the gun batteries on shore. The Congress' deck filled with dead and wounded, until at last she ran up the white flag of surrender.

Buchanan sent his gunboats alongside the Congress to accept

the surrender, to take prisoners and to burn the ship. At this point sharpshooters from the Union forces on shore opened fire on the gunboats. To find out why the burning was taking so long, Buchanan sent out his remaining lifeboat *(right)*. Before the boat reached the Congress the lieutenant in charge of it was wounded by a shot from shore. Now furious, Buchanan ordered his men to fire a "hot shot," a cannon ball heated red hot so that it would set the crippled vessel aflame. Then he excitedly snatched a carbine and went out on deck to return the annoying Union fire. But as he raised his gun, a sharpshooter's bullet hit him in the thigh. It was impossible for him to continue his command and Lieutenant Catesby Jones, the executive officer, took over. By now the hot shot had done its job: the Congress, burning brightly, would cause no more trouble.

Jones decided to go next after the warship Minnesota, which had run aground trying to reach the scene of action. Low tide and nightfall, however, were approaching, and the Merrimack's pilots refused to run the shallow channels under such conditions. So Jones broke off the attack and ordered his battered ship home. He would take care of the Minnesota the next morning.

When news of what the Merrimack had done reached Washington that night, panic set in. In a few hours the ironclad ship had routed a good part of the Union fleet. She had crushed the Cumberland's wooden hull like an eggshell. She had burned the Congress to the water's edge and driven the mighty Minnesota aground. It was the worst defeat the U.S. Navy had suffered up to that time. (Although the North did not know it, 21 of the Merrimack's men had been killed or wounded; she had lost her ram and she leaked badly.)

Navy Secretary Welles remained calm, assuring President Lincoln that the North's answer to the Merrimack, the Monitor, was on her way. Secretary of War Edwin Stanton, however, was furious when he heard that the little iron ship carried only two guns. He ordered 60 canal boats filled with rocks and sunk in the Potomac River to stop the Merrimack from sailing on Washington.

When the Monitor pulled into Hampton Roads at 10 o'clock that evening, her crew could see the fine old Congress still aflame. The Monitor reported to the Union flagship Roanoke. Her orders had changed: she was not going to Washington, but instead was to proceed immediately to the helpless Minnesota and protect her against another attack. The strange little ironclad ship did not inspire the crews of the other Union ships, who had seen what the Merrimack could do. To them the Monitor looked perhaps a quarter the Merrimack's size, and had only a fraction as many guns. What chance did she have?

As the Monitor pulled alongside the Minnesota, the Congress exploded *(left)*. No one on the Monitor spoke a word. A chill ran through every man.

When the Monitor pulled into Hampton Roads late on March 8, orders were relayed by shouting from man to man; the ship's speaking tube had been broken during the trip.

At 6 o'clock the next morning, the Merrimack appeared again from behind Sewell's Point, and started for the Minnesota to finish her job. But this time Jones discovered something new between him and his target—the North's "tin can on a raft."

At the same time the crew of the Union ironclad got their ship under way to head off the attack. Below deck, dimly lit by lanterns, everyone was at his post. The air was tense and still, for almost none of the crew could see the enemy. Only the captain, pilot and helmsman in the pilot house, peering through narrow slits in the armor, could watch the Merrimack approaching.

At last the silence was broken

by the crack of a single cannon, then a second and a third; shots whistled over the Monitor. The Minnesota's captain, having no confidence in his little protector, had opened fire on the Merrimack. Both ships were ricochet firing—skipping cannon balls along the water's surface in an attempt to hit the enemy near the waterline. The little Monitor was caught in between! As she moved in for her attack she was struck by shot from both sides.

As the Monitor headed out through the splash of cannon shot, Worden gave the order: "Commence firing!" Lieutenant Greene quickly forgot that he had not slept in 51 hours. Sweat poured from his brow as he fired the Monitor's first shot *(left)*. It bounced harmlessly off the Merrimack's slanting side.

For the next three hours the two ironclads slowly circled each other. The Monitor was able to load and fire only every 7 or 8 minutes, but nearly every shot hit its target, while the Merrimack's exploding shells did no damage to Ericsson's ironclad. Soon the effects of the battle began to show on the Merrimack. Almost everything on her deck had been shot away; her smokestack was riddled with holes and the draft in the furnaces was so bad that it was difficult to keep up steam.

Frustrated because his shells were bouncing harmlessly off the Monitor, Jones decided to ram, even though the Merrimack had lost her iron beak. In the Monitor, Worden waited, white-faced, for the blow; he had to see if his new iron ship could take it. As the bigger ship crashed into the Monitor's side *(next page)*, the latter's thick overhang absorbed the blow.

Worden, seeing his own chance, wheeled about and closed

in on the Merrimack. His decision to attack, however, was to prove a disastrous one. When the Monitor was only 20 yards away, Lieutenant John Taylor Wood, in charge of the Merrimack's stern rifle, lined up carefully on the pilot house *(left)*. The shot was perfectly aimed. A flash of light and a cloud of smoke filled the Monitor's tiny control center *(right)*. Captain Worden staggered and clapped his hands to his eyes as blood streamed from his powder-blackened face. "My eyes! I am blind!" he moaned. Worden was carried to his cabin, and Lieutenant Greene took command. During the confusion, the Monitor wandered aimlessly away from the battle.

On the Merrimack, crewmen cheered to see the Monitor apparently giving up the fight. Lieutenant Jones, thinking he had won a victory, headed his ship back toward Norfolk for repairs and a rest. In the Monitor, Greene at last gave an order to bring the ship about and return to battle. But by this time all he saw was the Merrimack limping away. Baffled by the Rebel's retreat, Greene headed back to what was left of the Union fleet. His orders were to save the Minnesota, and he had. The Monitor, too, had accomplished her mission.

The duel of the ironclads, which soon became famous around the world, had ended in a draw. Neither ship had clearly won, although victory was claimed by both sides. Almost immediately the arguments started. What if the Merrimack had concentrated fire on the Monitor's pilot house to destroy her control center? What if the Monitor, in turn, had concentrated on the Merrimack's waterline, where the armor was weakest? What if the Monitor had used 30-pound powder charges in her big guns, instead of the 15 pound charges strictly ordered by naval officials, who had not had a chance to test the guns? When Ericsson was told about this, he was furious. "If they had kept off at a distance of 200 yards and held her gun exactly level," he fumed, "the [30 pound charges] would have gone clear through." Even so, the little Monitor had proved her ability. She had hit the Merrimack 50 times, cracking six of the bigger ship's iron plates, and sent her home leaking. She had been hit only 21 times herself, and was virtually undamaged.

For the next two months the Monitor lay in Hampton Roads with the Union fleet. The Merrimack, after being repaired, appeared once more and cruised around inviting a fight. But President Lincoln had ordered the Monitor to stay away from the Southern ironclad because of what another battle might bring. There were still many people who were not convinced of the Monitor's ability.

At the beginning of May, orders came for Southern forces to evacuate Norfolk and Portsmouth, leaving those cities to advancing Union armies. To prevent her capture, the Merrimack's new commander, Commodore Josiah Tattnall, decided to lighten the heavy ship so she could pass up the shallow James River to Richmond, which was still in Southern hands. On his orders, the crew began to throw overboard everything they could move. But after hours of work they still could not make her light enough, so during the night of May 10-11 she was run aground and set on fire. When the flames reached her powder magazines, the Merrimack exploded. It was a sad end for a gallant ship.

The Monitor did not fare any better. In December she was ordered to sail down the coast to North Carolina to assist in the Union attack on Wilmington. But as she passed off Cape Hatteras around midnight on December 30, she foundered in a gale. The winds and rough seas were too much for the little iron boat. Her captain gave the order to abandon ship and the sea became her grave.

Although both ships saw only one major battle, they left lasting marks on history. The Merrimack, just by being where she was, had discouraged General McClellan from using the James River to move on Richmond. If he had, some historians believe, he might have taken the Southern capital quickly and ended a long, bloody war three years sooner than it actually did. It remained for General Grant, in 1865, to use the same basic plan to capture the city and force the South's surrender.

Most important, the two iron ships gave birth to modern navies. They had shown, once and for all, that wooden ships and sails were not enough. The Monitor's revolving turret became the basic weapon for warships everywhere, gradually leading to the huge battleships of many turrets that ruled the oceans for years—until more modern and still deadlier weapons made even these mighty monsters obsolete.

INDEX

ACKNOWLEDGMENTS

The artist and editors wish to thank the following: Rear Admiral George Dufek (U.S.N., ret.), Director of the Mariners Museum, Newport News, Va. and museum staff members Harold Sniffen, Mrs. Gerard P. Smith Jr., Robert Burgess, John Lochhead and William Radcliffe; Dr. Philip Lundeberg and William Geohagan of the Smithsonian Institution, Washington, D.C.; the Library of Congress; Marshall Butt of the Portsmouth Historical Association; John W. Porter; Alexander C. Brown, Chairman of the Newport News Historical Committee; and finally James Leftwich, of La Jolla, Calif. for ancillary research and for commenting on the manuscript.

ABOUT THE ARTIST

Fred Freeman, an ex-Navy Commander, has designed and illustrated many books, manuals and magazine articles on sea and space travel, including a *Picture History of the U.S. Navy,* with Theodore Roscoe, and Wernher von Braun's *First Men to the Moon.* He has received two medals from the Art Directors Club of New York.